GERALD FADAYOMI

BEFORE YOU GO

FOLLOWING JESUS
AND GROWING IN YOUR FAITH
AFTER HIGH SCHOOL

Before You Go
Published by Orange, a division of The reThink Group, Inc.
5870 Charlotte Lane, Suite 300
Cumming, GA 30040 U.S.A.

The Orange logo is a registered trademark of
The reThink Group, Inc.

All Scripture quotations, unless otherwise noted, are taken from the Holy
Bible, New International Version®. NIV®. Copyright © 1973, 1978, 1984 by
International Bible Society. Used by permission of Zondervan.

Other Orange products are available online and direct from the publisher. Visit
our website at www.ThinkOrange.com for more resources like these.

ISBN: 978-1-63570-081-7

Writers: Gerald Fadayomi
Contributors: Riley Reeves, Sam Short, Payton Richardson, Cole Wheeler,
Blake Eason, Luke Worteman, Madison Backus, Allison Norton,
Caleb Murphy, Lauren Ionta
Editing Team: Sarah Shelton, Nicole Bader Jones
Project Manager: Nate Brandt
Cover Design: The Cllctve
Interior Design: Donna Cunningham

Printed in the United States of America
First Edition 2018

4 5 6 7 8 9 10 11 12 13

07/01/2020

DEDICATION

This book is dedicated to my mentor, friend, and brother Wesley Bender. Thank you for believing in me when no one else did. For showing me what it truly means to follow Jesus and for praying for me, since my freshman year in high school. Because of your investment in me, I know Jesus today.

My Prayer is that your investment will be multiplied in every student that reads this book and as a result his or her faith will continue in college.

FOREWORD

BY CLAY SCROGGINS

Ten years ago.

That was the first time I heard the name, Gerald Fadayomi.

Now, of course, you don't just forget a name like that, but that's not why I remember hearing his name. In 2009, I was sitting at a coffee shop with a friend of mine named Wes, who was the National Director of all the YMCA Teen Programs. Wes was, and is, one of the sharpest youth leaders I've ever been around. Because of my respect for Wes and because of the growth that was happening in student ministry at our church, I asked him a simple question: "Do you have any names of youth speakers that would be willing and interested in speaking to our students?"

Not only did Wes answer my question, but he also took it one step further. I'll never forget the certainty and confidence in his response and the wry smile on his face as he said, "Yes, I do. In fact, I'll give you the name of the best speaker to high school students I've ever heard. And once you hear him, he'll be the best you've ever heard too…His name is Gerald Fadayomi."

Because I tend to be more cynical than naïve, I thought, "That's sweet, Wes. He might be the best you've ever heard, but I highly doubt he'll be the best I've ever heard." And as you're reading this, I'm sure you're thinking the same thing. I don't blame you. As recently as last week, I sat in the back of an arena filled with students and church leaders listening to Gerald speak for the hundredth time and I thought about this story. Turns out, I was wrong. Wes was right.

You see, Gerald is more than just a skilled orator. He's more than just an engaging communicator. He's more than just a terrific storyteller.

Gerald is a man on a mission. Once you read his story, you'll understand what I mean. He's a deep well, but his well wasn't dug out by academia or even by ministry. Gerald's well is deep, because his experience is so completely unique. His life experiences have created for him a depth that very few people his age have.

However, it's not just the depth of his soul that makes him great. No, he could've filled that crater with bitterness, rage, anger, or any other negative emotion, but that's not Gerald. He's worked as hard as anyone I've ever met to become a healthy, God-fearing, Jesus-loving, compassionate, kind-hearted, thoughtful leader. Life has created a deep well for Gerald, but he's allowed God to fill him with a Christ-likeness spirit that makes him a powerful force as a speaker and a writer.

For the last decade, people have told Gerald that he needs to put his story to paper and I couldn't be more excited that he finally has. He could've done it in so many different forms, but even the way he's decided to get his story out to the world speaks to his character and passion. *Before You Go* is a fantastic concept driven by a fantastic person.

There's an epidemic in the global church. Too many students are walking away from Christianity after high school. They're not just leaving our churches, but worse, they're leaving their own faith. Colleges, universities, and emerging adulthood are swallowing them up, spitting them out, and leaving them faithless.

Before You Go is definitely not **THE** solution, but it's certainly part of the solution. We're all aware of the problem and we've all got stories to tell. Fortunately, this book is not a diagnosis of the problem. Far better than just a diagnosis, this book is one of the best resources for any student moving on to the next season of life. This book is profoundly practical, wonderfully helpful, super interesting, and deeply rooted in Gerald's own personal story.

You don't just need to read it for yourself, but you need to do whatever you can do to get it in the hands of every high school graduate within your sphere of influence. At this point, there's too much at stake to leave anything on the table. The good news is that once anyone picks up this book, they won't be able to put it down. You might have the whole seat, but you'll only need the edge of it!

Our church is behind this book because our church is behind Gerald. We need more leaders like Gerald, shaping and leading the next generation. If you aren't already convinced of this, you will be after you read this book. As you're helping students pack their bags for the next season, make sure this book gets packed. They'll need it. And I promise you they'll be so glad they have it!

PREFACE

Q: Hey, someone gave me this book and told me I should
read it before I graduate high school. But I've literally
never heard of you, and honestly, books aren't really
my thing. Why should I read this?

A: I'm nobody important but let me tell you my story.
We can just go from there.

Both of my parents are African. Now, when I say African, I don't
mean African-American; I mean African-African. My dad is
from Nigeria, and his name is OluwaFemi. My mom is from
Liberia. Her name is Ekua. Somehow the two came together
and had a kid by the name of Gerald (which ironically, is like the
whitest name ever). I'll be honest, I'm grateful for it, because they
easily could have named me something like Mufasa. *That* would
have made for an interesting childhood. Well actually, interesting
might be the perfect word to describe the way I grew up. My
parents were never married and because of that there was a lot of
inconsistency in my life.

I don't know how far back into your childhood you can
remember, but my earliest childhood memories start right around
five years old. One of my earliest memories is of standing in
line with my mom outside of this strange building. It was late
at night and I remember feeling nervous. I didn't know where

we were or what was going on, but I remember my mom being really happy when we got inside. I, on the other hand, was totally confused. Inside, I remember seeing bunk beds all over the room, and it was filled with people I had never seen before. I didn't know how to respond. That's probably because my mom didn't really explain what was happening at the time. But as I think about that night now, I know exactly what was happening. That was the first night I spent in a homeless shelter.

I can't tell you how many nights we spent there or even where we went after that; it's all a bit of a blur. The next clear childhood memory I have is of my mom and I walking through an apartment complex knocking on doors to find an old friend of hers. It was hot and I was tired of walking, but we finally found her friend's apartment… or so I thought. What actually happened was that for several weeks we lived with some lady we didn't know who felt bad when she saw my mom struggling to take care of me. Now I know what you're thinking, *That's crazy.* And it was. But there is something you should know about my mom: She has schizophrenia. Obviously, I didn't know that as a five-year-old boy, and I actually didn't even find out until I was in my early twenties. But knowing that now, helps me make sense of the things that happened in my childhood.

After a few weeks of living with this random lady, we had to move out. My mom went to our church to try and get us some help. They were kind enough to put us up in a hotel for the night, and it was the best sleep I had in a long time. That dream didn't last for long though. The next morning, I woke up to a loud knocking at the door. Panicked, my mom quickly told me to hide under the bed. When she opened the door, the police burst into our hotel room. Two large hands dragged me out from under the bed, put me in the back of a cop car, and delivered me right to foster care.

I remember it like it was yesterday. You see, when my mom went to our church for help, they knew that the best way to help us was to move me away from an environment that wasn't safe. At the time, my mom just wasn't in a place to take care of me. The irony of the moment is that Mary J. Blige's "I'm Not Gonna Cry" was playing on the radio while I was in the back of this cop car bawling my eyes out, not knowing where I was going, where my mom was, or what was going to happen to me.

I didn't end up staying in foster care for too long. Unbeknownst to me, my mom and dad were in the middle of a custody fight that my dad eventually won. He'd recently gotten married, so when he gained custody of me, we moved in with his new wife to a little suburb in Michigan called Big Rapids. And to be honest, things in Michigan weren't half bad. It took a little while for me to get comfortable and make friends, but after a while, I was right at home.

It was in Michigan that I developed a love for basketball. Of course, this was partially because I thought I was the next LeBron, but mostly because it was the only sport I knew of that you could play inside under the comfort of air conditioning. But after a couple years in Michigan, my mom got back on her feet, gained custody of me again, and moved me back to Atlanta. And during that time with her, things really were a lot better. I made some pretty good friends, played a ton of basketball, and was doing pretty well in school. I mean, we didn't have a lot of money and I didn't dress as nice as some of the kids in my school, but for the most part, we were happy.

And then high school came along. My freshmen and sophomore years were relatively normal. I split most of my time between school, basketball, and hanging out at the YMCA.

But if you can remember back to your year as a junior, then you don't need me to tell you that things got hard when I hit that junior year. You're prepping for college with the SATs and ACTs and studying through some of your hardest classes in high school. All the work you do for school makes that third year of high school so challenging, but for me, it was a different kind of challenge. Junior year was difficult for me, because it was the year that I got the phone call that would change the rest of my life.

I remember it vividly. I was sitting on the couch around 9:00 at night when the phone rang. When I answered, I could hear the nervousness in my mom's voice on the other line. She told me she wouldn't be coming home that night, but that I didn't need to worry because she would be back the next day. Well, that day turned into a month. Then, that month turned into a year. And eventually, that year turned into three years. You see, my mom's disease had gotten the worst of her again, and it led her to make some bad decisions—the kind of decisions that landed her in jail.

There I was, a 17-year-old boy trying to figure out this thing called life on my own. Here's the thing: I had grown up in the church. Right before my sophomore year, I made the decision to become a Christian. But once my mom ended up in jail, things changed.

My mom was a Christian, and I remember thinking that if this is what it meant to be a Christian, then I was out. I wanted nothing to do with it. Because if God could allow something like this to happen to my mom and me, then He wasn't the kind of God I wanted anything to do with anymore.

This was a moment in my life that would shape my perspective for a long time. When you're suddenly a teenager with no parents, you start to see the world a little bit differently. It's hard to trust people. You feel so out of control that you want to take things into your own hands. And for me, it made it really hard to believe in God.

From there, I bounced between the homes of family members and friends, until I eventually landed at my grandmother's house in Norcross, Georgia. I didn't have any contact with my dad so that was my best option. I finished up high school there and decided I didn't want to go to college. I'd run into some friends of mine who were throwing parties for a living, so I started hanging out with them, learning the "business," and eventually ended up becoming a club promoter in Atlanta. I did that for three years with some friends of mine, and we actually became pretty good at it. We threw parties in pretty much every club in the city and if I'm being honest, I loved it. We were partying, smoking, drinking, making decent money, and had a lot of girls around us. And for the first time in my life, I felt accomplished, popular, and like I mattered. In the dimly lit rooms of those clubs, my perspective was still being shaped.

In the third year of club promoting, things took a turn for the worse. I watched three of my friends die from hanging around the club scene. They didn't just die; they were murdered. If that wasn't enough to shake me up, later that same year, a friend of mine took his own life. It was so much loss that it caused me to really start questioning a lot of things in my life. So that summer, instead of sticking with the club scene, I ended up back at the YMCA at a camp called Mission: Atlanta. For that week of camp, I led a group of students serving kids in impoverished neighborhoods. The YMCA had no idea what I was actually doing with my life at the time. Because if they did, there is no way they would have let me lead those students. But I'm so thankful they gave me a chance, because it was during that week that a mom of one of the students I was leading said something to me that would forever change the trajectory of my life.

She said, "Man, I wish my son had someone like you around him more often."

I remember thinking, *No you don't. Lady, you have no idea who I am, and if you did, you wouldn't be saying that to me.* But I couldn't shake that statement off. It made me think a lot about my life. And later that week, it had me lying on the floor of the YMCA in tears trying to process what it might mean for the rest of my life. I looked over at my friend—one of the club guys I'd

convinced to come with me to this camp—and told him we had
to quit throwing parties. Just like that. It had to be different.
The next morning, I found my friend Sam and told her what
was going on. She looked at me and said, "Gerald, I don't know
what to tell you, but you need to listen to this song." It was "How
He Loves" by David Crowder. I listened to the song but was so
confused by the opening line.

He is jealous for me.

I didn't get that. Why would God be jealous for a guy like me?
My dad didn't want me. It felt like my mom abandoned me. And
just look at all the things I had done wrong over the last three
years of my life. Not only that, I had abandoned God. I turned
my back on God. I gave up on Him. To me, there was no way
God could even still want me, let alone be jealous for me.

But the strangest thing started to happen. The
more I listened to that song, the more I heard
about the love God had for me. And because of
that, my perspective of God started to change.
And the more that perspective changed, the
more I began to believe that everything the
song said about God and the way He felt about
me was true.

That song led me to David Crowder's Pandora station (*Spotify*
wasn't a thing yet, you guys). I started listening to more Christian

music, reading my Bible, and eventually, that song led me back to church. I remember going there and seeing people actually sing the songs that I had heard on Pandora. And not just sing them, but really mean what they were saying. I remember being shocked when we got out of church in just an hour; that was way different than the church I had grown up in! Most of all, I remember walking out and feeling like I could do something with what I just heard.

I kept coming back. Sunday after Sunday, I showed up. And in January of 2011, I made a decision to give my life back to Jesus. I made a decision to follow Him. And this time, it was different. This time, I wasn't going to let anything change my perspective on who I knew God really was.

Fast-forward seven years and here I am as a student pastor at one of the largest churches in America. I wouldn't have ever imagined this for myself, but by the grace of God, I have the chance to invest my life into the lives of some of the greatest students in the world. I learn so much just by being with them, and every now and then, I think they learn a little bit from me, too. I love that so much! I love that I can learn from these students, and that I can pour into them the things I have learned along the way.

And on February 9, 2018, I had a night where I experienced both of those moments in a way that I'll never forget. Night One of our spring retreat was officially complete. Nine hundred students had exited the building and were headed to host homes all over the community to spend the night with their friends before returning to the church the next morning. As I walked the halls of our church, I noticed one of my favorite (yes, student pastors have favorites) former students standing there in a bright yellow "Event Team" t-shirt. He was volunteering for the weekend with some of our other recent graduates and was about to head back to his parents' basement for the night.

Now because he was a college student, I knew he appreciated two things: cheap food and late nights. I invited him and a few others to Waffle House that night. (Because no place is better for cheap food and late nights than Waffle House, you guys.) What was meant to just be a good hang quickly turned into a deeper conversation about college and faith. Before I knew it, I was pouring my heart out to these students. I was telling them all of the things that I wished someone would have told me when I finished high school. Things that might have kept me from going down the path I went down those years after graduation. Things that might have helped me avoid making some of the decisions I made. Things that wouldn't prevent living with some of the regrets I have now.

This conversation with those seven college freshmen led me to write this book. After sitting with them for two hours, I spent the whole drive home processing everything we'd just talked about. And I kept coming back to this thought: *Man, I wish we'd had that conversation before they graduated.* I started thinking about the 200 seniors at my church right now, and how much I wanted to have that same conversation with them right where they are now—before they're in the midst of college life.

So when I got home, I opened the notes app on my phone, sat in my car, and started writing. And when I was done, I was left with a list of ten. Ten ideas, ten thoughts, ten things I want every high school senior (including you!) to know before they go on to the next stage of their life.

Now before we get to that, here is what I know about you. You are busy. You have senioritis. You are definitely tired of reading. You don't really need another book. What you really need is the CliffsNotes version (because that's how you got through high school anyway). Well, consider this your CliffsNotes version! Instead of taking these ten thoughts and stretching them out into hundreds of pages, I decided to keep it simple. Ten thoughts, 132 pages, and you're done!

In these pages, you'll read letters written from those same college freshmen I talked with that night. You'll hear an explanation from me of some of their thoughts, and I'll even give you a few questions to process along the way. My hope is that this short(er) book will give you some things to think about, allow you some time to process, and help prepare you for what is ahead. I hope that this will help you avoid some of the avoidable hurt, pain, and drama that comes with life after high school. And I hope that it will challenge and stretch you. But most of all, I hope that it will help you grow your faith, find community, and build your relationship with God in a brand-new way!

So, pack up your bags, hug your parents goodbye and let's jump in!

Because before you go, you should know....

CHAPTER
ONE

Q: I go to church every Sunday. Why do I need to read another book about it?

A: Well, you have gotten this far and you're still reading it so that has to be a good sign, right? So, while I have you here, let me tell you why I believe there is a difference between loving Jesus and going to church.

Dear Future College Student,

You are in the process of completing or have just completed a huge chapter in your story: high school. This season of your life is a whirlwind of emotions and an important time to reflect on the last four years that have just flown by. While you're frantically fighting to hold onto this time with friends, you're also trying to gather up the necessary tools to survive the unknown territory of college ahead.

Change is big, exciting, and sometimes downright terrifying. I get it. But I'm here to assure you of one change that may seem scary in the beginning but can actually be an incredible blessing for your college experience.

If you are involved with a church and consider it your second home, then I guarantee that finding a church in your college town is probably at the top of your to-do list. And it should be! But I just want to be the first to say that although finding a place to worship or a Christian community is great, it's not the most important thing. Realizing this was difficult for me when I attended a school outside of Georgia. I thought I needed to find a church and surround myself with good Christian people to be a devout Jesus follower. I thought that if I wasn't involved with a Christian organization, then I wasn't doing my best to serve His Kingdom. After a couple of weeks though, God opened my eyes. I began to realize that my love for Him isn't and shouldn't be confined to a Sunday church service. It lives within our soul and is meant to touch everyone we come into contact with, both inside and outside the walls of a church.

Before college, pray that the Lord would strengthen your relationship with Him. Pray that He would introduce you to a child in need of their Heavenly Father. Understand that you are the church. I am the church. We are qualified to love others the way Christ calls us to love. Invite Jesus into your college experience and watch His miracles unfold through you.

Cheering YOU on,

Lauren Tonta

When I was six-years-old, my dad gave me the most incredible present. I remember coming down the stairs on Christmas morning and opening the perfectly wrapped gift to find a brand-new Super Nintendo inside. And to top it off, it was fully equipped with the game *Duck Hunt*. Man, I loved that game. I played it literally every day. I was obsessed with it!

But can you imagine if I became so consumed with the gift that I just stopped talking to my dad—the guy who gave it to me? What if I loved the gift so much, I just decided that if I wasn't playing *Duck Hunt* with my dad, then I wanted nothing to do with him. *Worst Son of All Time Award?* Well, the winner would be me!

For as long as you have attended your church, the pastor's goal has been to help you fall more in love with Jesus. They've worked really hard to create retreats, events, programming, Bible studies, sermons, small groups, and more to accomplish that one, specific goal. And that's amazing!

But the danger is that, as a result of all those experiences, you sometimes come to love your *church* more than you love Jesus.

I know that sounds crazy, but it's true. If you could never imagine going to another church, listening to another pastor, or growing in your relationship with Jesus without the safety net of the church you currently attend, then you are focusing on the wrong thing. Let me be clear: I want you to love your church! I just don't want you to build your faith around it. Because when you do, that faith will fall apart when you leave it. The reality is, where you attend church now probably won't be where you attend when you leave for college or move on to whatever is next for you. In fact, there may not even be a church like the one you attend now anywhere near where you're headed next. But I want you to pursue Jesus either way.

Think about this. Jesus' disciples had no church to attend. Or at least, they had no church building to attend. What they did have was each other. They had the stories of their time with Jesus, and the experiences they shared alongside Him. I mean, they saw Him rise from the dead together! I think it's safe to say that was enough to bond them for life.

The disciples were so blown away by God's love for them demonstrated through the life of Jesus that they put their lives on the line to prove their love for Him. Look at the conversation Peter and John had with the people who literally crucified Jesus just weeks before:

> *The priests and the captain of the temple guard and the Sadducees came up to Peter and John while they were speaking to the people. They were greatly disturbed because the apostles were teaching the people, proclaiming in Jesus the resurrection of the dead. They seized Peter and John and, because it was evening, they put them in jail until the next day. But many who heard the message believed; so the number of men who believed grew to about five thousand.*

The next day the rulers, the elders and the teachers of the law met in Jerusalem. Annas the high priest was there, and so were Caiaphas, John, Alexander and others of the high priest's family. They had Peter and John brought before them and began to question them:

"By what power or what name did you do this?"
Then Peter, filled with the Holy Spirit, said to them: "Rulers and elders of the people! If we are being called to account today for an act of kindness shown to a man who was lame and are being asked how he was healed, then know this, you and all the people of Israel: It is by the name of Jesus Christ of Nazareth, whom you crucified but whom God raised from the dead, that this man stands before you healed. Jesus is 'the stone you builders rejected, which has become the cornerstone.' Salvation is found in no one else, for there is no other name under heaven given to mankind by which we must be saved."

When they saw the courage of Peter and John and realized that they were unschooled, ordinary men, they were astonished and they took note that these men had been with Jesus.
- Acts 4:1-13 -

There were no bands, no student space, no flashing lights, and no photo booths. Their lives were on the line, and still, their faith was strong and growing every day. Now, I'm not saying you have to risk your life to prove your love for God, but I am saying

Jesus, in and of Himself, should be enough for us to continue following Him.

Even if you can't find a church like the one you have now, you can still find Jesus.

So, what would it look like for you to start thinking about your relationship with God differently? What would it look like for your faith to be fueled by your love for Jesus? What would it look like for you to pursue Him even when it's hard?

I wrote a few questions for you to ask yourself that I hope will help you clarify why you love Jesus. I hope they will guide you toward continuing to pursue your relationship with Him as you move on to the next season of your life.

QUESTIONS

1. Why do you love Jesus?

_____

_____

_____

_____

_____

2. What does a personal relationship with Him look like
    for you?

_____

_____

_____

_____

3. What is the best time of day for you to connect with
    God? Why?

_____

_____

_____

_____

_____

4. How do you best connect with God? (For example, worship
    music, reading Scripture, journaling, etc.)

_____

_____

_____

_____

_____

_____

_____

ACTION STEP

Use your answers and pick a time each day to spend 15 minutes
with God. During that time, take 10 of those minutes to connect
with Him the way that you connect with Him best. Then, take
the last five minutes to pray and thank God for the day.

CHAPTER
TWO

Q: Okay, so what are all the things I need to stop doing to prove that I love Jesus? I mean, have you seen my Insta bio with the Christian worship lyrics in it?

A: Well, it's not about what you don't do; it's about what you do do. (And yes, I know I said do do. You're about to graduate high school; get it together!)

Dear Future College Student,

I just wanted to start this little letter by encouraging you to really try and make the most of high school. I know friendships can be difficult, family can be aggravating, and the idea of getting out of it all can seem like the biggest breath of fresh air. And to an extent, it is. College is incredible and has been one of the most fruitful, humbling, and exciting seasons of my life. With that being said, be excited because it's such a fun season, but stay present. Make the most of what's left of high school. It's cliché, but it really is going to go by way faster than you think.

For me (and I think the vast majority of other college freshmen), this year has been a combination of some of the most exciting and spontaneous moments I've ever had, but also some of the hardest and most confusing days I've ever lived. For a lot of us, this is the first time that we've been able to truly make a lot of choices on our own. We get to be in control of the majority of our lives. We decide what church we want to go to, what clubs and ministries we want to take part in, what people we want to surround ourselves with and most importantly, what kind of lives we want to live. In the midst of all this newfound freedom, the truths of Christianity can feel a lot more like rules and being a disciple can feel a lot like an obligation. But, if I have learned anything in the last six months, it's that the rules and the obligations aren't what it's about.

It is so easy to over-complicate the Gospel, but in the end, it really is just about the way we love the people around us and the way we love the God that has given us those people. You would be surprised how much falls into place when you just focus on love.

As soon as you start to center your days around simply knowing more about Jesus and caring for the people that have been placed in your life, not only does a massive weight and pressure get lifted, you truly start to feel the fresh air you were intended to breathe in.

So, if I can leave you with anything, it's to forget the "don'ts" that have become so pressing in our culture and set your eyes on the "do's." Get in the word, befriend God (because He wants to be your friend!), be kind, and love well. There will be hard seasons. There will be confusion. Honestly, there's a good chance there will be doubt. Stand firm, love well, and don't stop pursuing.

Keep the Gospel simple, and just like Hosea 6:3 says, "He will come to you like the rain."

I'm rooting for you!

Riley Reeves

You know who used to drive me crazy when I was playing basketball growing up? Referees. Man, they drove me nuts. It seemed like every time we lost a basketball game it was because of the refs. (In actuality it was because our team was terrible, but that is not the point). Honestly, it wasn't even the losing that frustrated me. It was more the feeling that there were these people in every game whose only job was to watch my every move, wait for me to mess up, and then call out something I did wrong.

What's funny is that I remember when I first became a Christian, I sort of used the Bible like a referee's handbook. I knew that I had some things in my life that I needed to stop doing, so I used the Bible as my rule book to help me know when I was messing up. And honestly, maybe this is how you view the Bible, too. The problem is that this perspective paints an inaccurate picture of God. When we see the Bible as a rulebook, we start to see God as a referee. We see Him as someone who just watches and waits for us to mess up so He can blow the whistle and throw a flag on the play.

Let me let you in on a secret. That is not God. He isn't out to get us. He isn't waiting for you to mess up so He can punish you, and He isn't sitting in heaven surprised when we fall short. So, the question is this: If that isn't God, then what is God actually like?

That is a great question. I know, because I asked it myself!

In Colossians 1:15, Paul actually refers to Jesus as the visible image of the invisible God. And Paul's point is this: If you want to know what God is like, look to Jesus. If you want to know how God sees people, look to Jesus. If you want to know God's expectations for you, look to Jesus. And if you want to know how God feels when we mess up, look to Jesus.

What's interesting is that when we do this, we find out that Jesus was far more concerned with the do's than the don'ts of our faith. In fact, when Jesus was asked what the most important commandment is, He answered very clearly:

> *'Love the Lord your God with all your heart and with all your soul and with all your mind.' This is the first and greatest commandment. And the second is like it: 'Love your neighbor as yourself.' All the Law and the Prophets depend on these two commandments.*
> *- Matthew 22:37-40 -*

When Jesus said this, He meant the don'ts actually fall under two do's. I know that might be confusing, so let me expand.

Love God. Love your neighbor. That's it. Those are the do's.

The important thing about faith isn't a list of all the things we aren't supposed to do, but rather just this list of two things God wants us to do. Because if we were to do those two very simple things, everything else will fall into place. Here is what's even crazier. When Jesus said these two commands, what He was implying is that our love for others is as important as our love for God. The evidence of our love for God is actually demonstrated in our love for others. And if we make it our business to do this one thing really well, then we are fulfilling the greatest commandment God gave us.

I don't know about you, but I think that is really good news. It means that each day, you really only have one thing to worry about: Love. You know that trying to keep up with the don'ts is exhausting, frustrating, and really just impossible. So here is my challenge to you: Focus on the do's. Focus on loving the people around you well and honoring God with your life. And the rest? It will all fall into place!

QUESTIONS

1. What are some things you think being a Christian means you don't do?

_____

_____

_____

_____

_____

2. If you focused your energy on loving God and loving the people around you, would you do those things? Why or Why not?

_____

_____

_____

_____

_____

3. Who are some people who are difficult for you to love?

_____

_____

_____

_____

_____

4. What would it look like for you to love them?

_____

_____

_____

_____

_____

ACTION STEP

Each day when you wake up, ask yourself this question: "How can I love the people around me well today?" Then try and do it!

CHAPTER
THREE

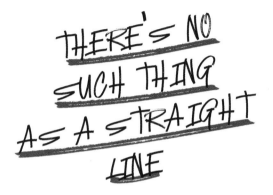

Q: I do love Jesus, but I'm afraid that when I get to college I am going to make a mistake. What if I royally screw this all up?

A: Well, have you ever drawn in a straight line? No? You know why you haven't? Because it's not possible to do it on your own.

Dear Future College Student,

You know that frustration when you're drawing out a chart for class or sketching a picture, and you can never seem to draw your lines perfectly straight? Even when you use a ruler, it somehow still goes wrong! It's so close to being perfect, but it's just not quite there. That's kind of how I view my freshman year of college. I had this straight and narrow daydream of how it was going to play out: I would immediately have a brand-new group of best friends, classes would actually be applicable to real life (still waiting on that), and God would just hand it all to me easily. You always hear, "College is the greatest four years of your life!" But what people neglect to tell you is that there are difficult realities every college student will face at one point or another.

This is in no way intended to be discouraging, because college is SO exciting and a pivotal moment in your life. I only say all of this to bring to your attention that there really is no such thing as a straight line. Truly, I wish there was. Life would be so much easier and less stressful that way. But if life were that way, there'd also be no room for God in your story. There'd be no real desire to crave His presence in your life.

As you enter this exciting, new season of life, I beg you to do one thing: Please do not compare your path to the path of people around you. College is a whole new world. The people you've known and been around your entire life are going to have a completely different experience than you, and that's okay! I have personally struggled to remember this as my freshman year has gone on and not exactly unfolded the way I thought it would.

Don't get me wrong; I love where I'm at, and God has been so faithful this year. But it didn't play out exactly like the daydreams I created in my head.

Maybe you've been waiting on this day for what feels like forever, and you can hardly wait to meet new people, see new places, and encounter a new freedom. Or maybe you're like I was. You're comfortable, you love the life you've so tirelessly built with the people around you, and the thought of that not being your reality anymore is terrifying.

Regardless of where you stand, please know that what God brings you into, He will faithfully bring you through. If you let Him, He will use you, teach you, and grow you in a way that you could have never fully imagined. Try to forget the stereotypes because every college experience looks different, and I pray that you allow God to use yours in incredible ways.

Go get 'em,

Payton Richardson

Somewhere along the way, we (well-meaning church and youth pastors, of course) have painted a picture that your faith should grow in a straight line. I've heard way too many stories of students who have either left the church or given up on following Jesus because of this misconception. So, let me take a second to set the record straight (pun intended). There is no such thing as a straight line when it comes to your relationship with God. It does not exist! It is not even Biblical to think that's the case. Should your faith be continually growing? Absolutely! But should it grow in a straight line? Absolutely not! Why? Because, that isn't the way relationships work, and Jesus came to offer us a relationship.

By now you've lived enough life to know that relationships are messy. They take time to grow. They have ups and downs. They ebb and flow. You get angry, you get stagnant, you have mountaintop moments and seasons in the valley, you have moments of joy and moments of frustration. And it is in each of those moments that you grow closer to God. Through all those seasons, you learn to trust Him, even when you can't understand what He is doing in your life. It's in both the highs and the lows that God is working to grow your faith.

Understanding this concept will change the way you respond when the high of summer camp fades and you suddenly don't feel as close to God. Understanding this will allow you to walk back into the church after you've made a mistake in your life. It will free you up to enjoy your growth and experience a true relationship with God. And to be completely honest, until we understand that there is no such thing as a straight line, we'll

never fully understand God's grace. Straight-line thinking
makes us believe that if we are good enough, we can earn right
standing with God. But grace reminds us that right standing
with God isn't something we can earn. We can't possibly do that
on our own.

I love the way Paul wrote about grace in Ephesians:

> *For it is by grace you have been saved, through faith—*
> *and this is not from yourselves, it is the gift of God—*
> *not by works, so that no one can boast.*
> *- Ephesians 2:8-9 -*

I love this because Paul described grace as a gift. You remember
the Super Nintendo we talked about earlier? I did nothing to
earn that gift. I did nothing to deserve it. I just received it. And
that is what grace is all about! It's about us getting to have a right
standing with God without doing anything to earn or deserve it.
We just receive it because of what Jesus did on the cross for you
and for me.

So, what does that all mean? Well, it means that even when you
slip up, God still loves you. It means that even when you fail,
God still cares about you. It means that even when you miss your
quiet time, God still wants to talk to you. It means that we don't
have to be perfect; we just have to be pursuing Him with all we
have. Quit chasing perfection; quit worrying about keeping up
with a straight-line relationship with God. Start enjoying the
moments you get to experience with your Heavenly Father.

QUESTIONS

1. What does having a relationship with God mean to you?

_____

_____

_____

_____

_____

2. Make a list of all the moments you have had with God over the last four years.

_____

_____

_____

_____

3. How have you grown in your relationship with God over the last four years?

_____

_____

_____

_____

ACTION STEP

Write a letter to yourself celebrating how far you've come since your freshman year of high school and thinking about how you want to grow in your relationship with God in this next season of your life. Leave the letter in your room at home and read it when you come back from school on break. If you do this, you will start to recognize how God is working in your life— how He is always pursuing you and wants you to be growing in your relationship with Him. Even if that means the line between you and Him isn't always straight!

CHAPTER
FOUR

LEARN TO MAKE NEW FRIENDS NOW

Q: Love Jesus. Grow in my faith. Okay, I think I can handle that! To be honest, what I'm really stressed about is leaving all my friends and moving to a new place. I mean, how do I even meet new people? Should I just start following a bunch of random people who are going to my college on Insta? That seems 100% creepy.

A: No, I wouldn't suggest becoming a stalker, but I would recommend you learning how to make new friends. And I mean real, live friends, not social media. I know, I know, but trust me, it's possible!

Dear Future College Student,

During your freshman year of college, you will meet more people than you have met in your entire life. Sometimes you will forget a person's name right after you meet them. The best part of it all is that you might find some of your best friends in the process. You may not even know it when you meet them! Learning how to meet new people and make new friends is a crucial part to being in college. But while you are meeting all these new people, it doesn't mean finding new friends will be easy. There is no "how-to" manual to making new best friends. (Trust me, I would have found it.) But there is still time in our day-to-day lives to step out of our comfort zones and meet someone new. Making new friends is going to require you to find the time to be intentional with the people you meet and the friends you have.

This may sound like a box to check off after you have met one person and made a new friend, but the reality is we are put in positions to meet and form new relationships all the time. What's crazy is you might cross paths with someone every day that you have a lot in common with, but you don't know because you've never actually spoken to them. So try this: Talk to some new people. And when you do, what you might find is that they were just as nervous as you were about making new friends.

Practice meeting a new person. Ask them about their family and what they love to do. And start now! Don't wait until college. Making new friends begins in the present.

Don't be afraid to step out of your comfort zone right where you are now. It will set you up for a college experience that you'll never forget.

Your friend,

Caleb Murphy

Think about your current friendships. How did you become friends? Where did you meet? Here is what I would be willing to bet: Your friends just sort of happened to you. Don't get me wrong, you love them, and they are probably great friends. My point is that you most likely didn't choose them. Those friendships came into your life pretty easily.

Let me explain. You probably became friends as a result of your parents knowing each other first. Or they were sitting next to you in your first period class when you got to high school. Or maybe you became friends through your small group at church. Whatever it was, there's a good chance your friendships happened based on circumstances in your life and comfort zone. For some of you, that worked out great, but for others, not so much.

The good news is that as you move into the next chapter of your life, you have an incredible opportunity ahead: You get to choose your friends! You have the power to choose the people who will walk through this next season of your life with you. Some of these people will even become your forever friends. But the problem here is that up until this point in your life, you may not have had the opportunity to really learn what it is like to make new friends. Your friendships just happened, and now here you are. You and your friends have the longest Snapchat streak of all time. Friends forever!

But now, friendships are about to change for you. Things are about to get real.

As I sat with this group of college freshmen at Waffle House that night, one of the things I heard over and over was how hard it was for them to make new friends. They knew how valuable community was as they started this new chapter, but they were struggling to find it. That's why I think it's so crucial for you to learn the skill of making new friends now!

You know who was really good at this? Wait for it... Jesus! I mean, what wasn't He good at, right? He is literally perf, you guys. Seriously though, what I love about Jesus is that He made friends with the least likely of suspects. Case in point, I love His interaction with a man named Zaccheaus. Here's this tax collector that is known for literally stealing from his family and friends, and Jesus still found a way to befriend him. (And He didn't even have insta-stalking to help him to do it!)

> *When Jesus reached the spot, he looked up and said to him,*
> *'Zacchaeus, come down immediately. I must stay at*
> *your house today.' So he came down at once and*
> *welcomed him gladly."*
> *- Luke 19:5-6 -*

Did you catch it? Jesus instantly won Zaccheaus over because He was willing to go where Zacchaeus was. He was willing to go to his house and have dinner with his friends. It's so simple. The context for this story is obviously a little different than you stepping onto a new college campus, but I think there is a principle in this story that we can still learn.

Let me start with what I am not saying. I am not saying that the way to make friends in college is to just do what everybody else is doing. I'm not saying you should go out drinking, or partying, or doing something you aren't sure about just so that you can make friends. What I am saying is that sometimes to make new friends, we have to get out of our comfort zones. We can't just wait for friends to come to us; we have to be intentional to go out and meet people ourselves. Maybe that means signing up for intramural sports, or joining a study group, or rushing a sorority or fraternity. You will have to use wisdom and discernment to figure out what opportunity is best for you. Meeting new people and making new friends won't come naturally; it will take effort on your part. But trust me when I tell you the effort will be worth it.

Here is what's cool about this. You don't have to wait! You don't have to wait until you find yourself at a new school in a new city. You can start now! At your school, in your community, and with some people you have never talked to before. Doing this will stretch you. It will teach you how to find common ground, how to ask for someone's number, and how to build great friendships. And all those things will help you as you make your way to college.

QUESTIONS

1. What is an activity or extracurricular that you have never participated in that you could try this year?

_____

_____

_____

_____

_____

2. What do you look for in a friend?

_____

_____

_____

_____

_____

3. What are three questions you could ask to get to know someone?

_____

_____

_____

_____

_____

ACTION STEP

The best way to meet new friends is through a shared activity. Try something new as a way to make new friends. It will require you getting out of your comfort zone, so use the answers to these questions as a way to help you identify what type of person would make a great friend for you and how you could get to know them once you meet them.

CHAPTER
FIVE

Q: Well, that helps me know where to start making new friends, but how can I make sure that my friends end up like, F.R.I.E.N.D.S?

A: I think I get what you're asking. What you want is an authentic community in an apartment in New York City with your five besties, living off coffee and takeout, right? Okay, but really, I do get it.

Dear Future College Student,

*At this point in your life, you are more than ready to leave your
hometown and start a new chapter in your life. You've probably heard
hundreds of people say that "college is the best four years of your life,"
and now you're finally ready to experience that for yourself. What
people don't tell you though, is that college is hard, and I'm not talking
about academically. Living in a new town is hard, not having your
mom take care of you when you're sick is hard, and making friends
is hard. You may have had the same friends since elementary school,
and at this point, you don't even remember how to make friends.
Don't become discouraged. The community that will surround you will
happen, and when it does, it will not be by mistake.*

*During the first semester of my freshman year in college, everybody
that I knew wanted to go out and party all the time. And I mean all
the time. I was in a very uncomfortable position being an 18-year-old
girl with a heart in pursuit of Jesus, but also wanting to be accepted
by this group of girls that were my new friends. For weeks I would go
downtown with these girls and get drunk, and I thought everything
was great and fun and going just as it should. Then I realized that the
only time they were asking to hang out with me was to go out. I took
a step back and noticed that I had been living only for myself and lost
sight of what our purpose on Earth is as Christians: to love everyone
we encounter and to spread the Gospel. I began to pray for my heart,
the community I had surrounded myself with, and the community I
would meet.*

*After about a week of diving into the Word, I knew what God wanted
me to do. The people I had been investing in for the past few months*

were not going to be my best friends, but they were still placed into my life for a reason. I began to ask them one by one to go to lunch so I could have more intimate time to connect with them. The more I talked with them, the more I realized that I was not the only one struggling with finding friendships that would make me better as a person.

Since I went out of my comfort zone and was obedient to what God wanted me to do, I became a leader in my community and in Christ.

I ended up inviting these girls to come to church with me on Wednesday nights and building relationships that I now hold close to my heart.

As you go into college, I encourage you to seek out opportunities to be a leader in the community you have found yourself in. Don't worry about if they're going to like you or look at you differently. Remember that you can make such a difference in someone's life that they will live for eternity, because you shared God's love onto them. Wishing you the best of luck as you begin this new chapter in your life.

With all my love,

Madi Backus

All the believers were together and had everything in common. Selling their possessions and goods, they shared with anyone who was in need. With one accord they continued to meet daily in the temple courts and to break bread from house to house, sharing their meals with gladness and sincerity of heart, praising God and enjoying the favor of all the people. And the Lord added to their number daily those who were being saved.

- Acts 2:44-47 -

Maybe this is just the pastor in me, but doesn't this sound a lot like the show *Friends*? They hung out together, they shared with each other, they ate together, they were always at each other's apartments, and they genuinely enjoyed each other's company. I doubt that this is where the concept of the show came from, but if we're honest, this kind of community is something all of us want. I mean, maybe not with a ton of people, but we all have a basic desire to belong. We want to know that we matter to someone else. And honestly, life just feels better when we aren't going through it alone. Community is important to all of us, but it's really difficult to find when you are just starting college.

Finding community is a lot like working out. Have you ever found yourself accidentally doing a push-up? Me either. You know why? Because no one works out by mistake. Even if you love working out, you still have to plan to do it. You have to set time aside and prioritize it. And if you really want to see the benefits of working out, you have to do it even when you don't feel like it. Finding community follows suit. It doesn't happen by mistake. You have to prioritize it and engage with people, even when you don't want to.

So, how do you find community? The answer is three simple words: location, intention, and vulnerability.

Location – Go to Christian places. This could be a local church, a student ministry on campus, a Bible study… you see where I'm going. Just find some places where there are people who believe what you believe. And trust me, they are out there. It just may require some effort from you to find them.

Intention – This one is easy to say but hard to do. Intention requires consistency and courage. You have to show up, not just once, but as often as you can for at least three months. That's right, three whole months. And when you show up, talk to people. Make an effort to engage with the people you meet. I know it's crazy, right?

Vulnerability – When I say vulnerability, I am not saying spill out your entire soul on day one. I am simply saying be yourself. Don't try too hard to fit in. Don't say things just because everyone else is saying them. When we do this, people don't get a chance to know the real us. Being real with other people is the first step in vulnerability. So, be your true self and let people get to know the real you. I promise they will like you. And if they don't? Well, they aren't your people.

Location, intention and vulnerability over time will lead you to authentic community. Don't be discouraged if it doesn't happen overnight. It will happen, but it will take some effort to get there.

QUESTIONS

1. Where do Christians meet at your college campus (church, clubs, college ministries, etc.)?

_____

_____

_____

_____

_____

2. What do you need to do to get involved in that environment?

_____

_____

_____

_____

3. What things about yourself are you afraid people will find out or see if you are vulnerable?

_____

_____

_____

_____

_____

4. What is the worst that could happen if they did?

_____

_____

_____

_____

_____

_____

ACTION STEP

Pick a place, club, or church and make a plan to attend consistently. Ask someone (an accountability partner, friend, roommate, etc.) to follow up with you in August and make sure you are working toward finding community at college.

CHAPTER
SIX

Q: Okay, Gerald, what is one thing I can do every day to keep growing?

A: Oh, that is an easy one! Pray for random people. That person you see all the time—the one you follow on Instagram, but you don't talk to in person? Yeah, I know that's a thing. Pray for that person.

Dear Future College Student,

College is hard. I often find myself asking God to carry me through the week, to help me focus in class, or to help me buckle down and get my homework done.

One common theme is that my prayers are all about me. In college, we tend to focus our prayers on ourselves and not on others because that's all our brains can afford to think about. But it's actually a breath of fresh air when you sit down with God and pray for someone else. It could be for a family member, someone who is sick, or even a total stranger. The idea is simply that your prayers are about more than just you. Praying for others allows you to take a step back from your own life and get a break from worrying about yourself. It makes you pay attention to the people around you, and it can potentially change someone's life.

Next time you see someone you may not know, ask them if you can pray for them. You never know what people are going through and having someone ask them if there is anything in their life you can pray for, can change that person's heart. It can let them know they're never out of God's reach. I don't expect you to approach someone random and go all "Jesus Loves You!" on them, but a simple, "Hey, do you mind if I pray for you today?" is feasible. In college, it's hard to look out for others when you can barely take care of yourself, so praying for others doesn't come naturally. But once a day when you're walking on campus and you see someone you know (or don't know!), say a simple prayer in your head that they have a good day or that they get through their week. You may not physically see any change that instant but, over time, God is working in your heart and theirs.

We live in a world where everyone worries about themselves, and as Christians, our job is to reflect Christ in the way we live. Be the difference in college and when people see you, make them ask, "What makes them so different?"

God bless and good luck!

Alli Norton

There are three words in the New Testament that really bother me, and they are found in 1 Thessalonians 5:

> *Rejoice always, pray without ceasing, give*
> *thanks in all circumstances; for this is the will*
> *of God in Christ Jesus for you.*
> *- 1 Thessalonians 5:16-18 -*

Rejoice always? That's hard, but I get what Paul is saying. There really is a lot to be grateful for in our lives. I mean, if you are reading this book right now, hopefully that means you are alive. That in and of itself is a reason to be grateful and rejoice! (It also means you paid for this book, therefore I am able to provide dinner for my family tonight, so really, thank you!)

Give thanks in all circumstances. Again, this is hard, but it makes sense. There is always a silver lining in every situation. It may be difficult to see in the hard moments of life. It may not even be that big of a silver lining, but there's always something to have gratitude for. I can see why Paul would say we should constantly give thanks to God, no matter our situation. It helps shape our attitude.

But the words that always tripped me up are the ones right in the middle of this verse: "Pray without ceasing." Every time I read that I think, *I don't have that much to pray about.* In about five minutes, I can ask for all the things I want. And if you give me a good ten minutes, I could ask for stuff that I don't even want, but just sounds cool to have.

In 2017, I heard a talk at a conference by a guy named Ryan Leak that rocked my world. It wasn't when he had me on the floor laughing at his jokes; it was when he switched gears and talked about how he started asking people if he could pray for them. When he said that, my mind was flooded with the people in my life that I could be praying for. At that moment, this idea of praying without ceasing didn't seem so impossible. And it shouldn't for you either!

Close your eyes and imagine this scenario. (Well, I guess you can't close your eyes and read at the same time, but imagine this with me anyway). A 27-year-old woman sits up in her room at 3 a.m. crying her eyes out. She has had the longest day at work. Her feet are aching from standing all day. Her 12-year-old son is failing two classes, and she has no idea what to do about it. She would ask her husband for help, but he is in the Army and away on his third deployment. She is exhausted. She is broken. She is hopeless. She was also your waitress at your favorite restaurant last night. I know that might seem dramatic, but that is actually someone's story. And what is even crazier is that we interact with people like this on a daily basis, yet we have no idea what their story is. We have no idea what's really going on in their lives.

Now, what if I told you that with just one sentence you could bring a smile to that woman's face? What if I told you with just one question you could give her a little hope? What if I told you with just seven words you could make a world of difference in her life? Wouldn't you want to do that? I'm sure you would! And the good news is, you can.

One of the things that I love so much about God is that He knows every person and every situation, yet He still allows us to present our requests to Him. He hears our prayers even about the smallest things and cares about what we have to say. So often as Christians, we leverage this incredible gift for our own benefit, and that's okay! But what if we decided to leverage it on behalf of the people around us as well? What if we were bold enough to simply ask the people we meet this simple question: How can I pray for you today?

I think we'd be surprised how quickly people would actually tell us how to pray for them. People may actually come to believe that there is a God who sees them and cares for them simply because there was a person who noticed them and cared enough to ask them this question. I think what might also happen is that you'll experience God grow and stretch you in new ways, too. That's what happens when He allows you to be a part of someone else's story. I think there is power in prayer, and I think there is beauty in praying for other people. When you do it, I think you will begin to notice that God is up to a lot more than you ever realized, and your faith will grow as a result.

QUESTIONS

1. What are the top three things you pray for on a regular basis?

_____

_____

_____

_____

_____

2. What would it look like for you to pray more consistently?

_____

_____

_____

_____

_____

3. Who can you pray for this week?

_____

_____

_____

_____

_____

ACTION STEP

Ask one person if you can pray for them today. Then, write down your prayer for them on this page.

_____

_____

_____

_____

_____

_____

_____

CHAPTER
SEVEN

GENEROSITY STARTS SMALL

Q: Pray? Okay, I think I can handle that. I was nervous you were going to ask me to do something hard like give my money away or something.

A: Well, now that you've brought it up...

Dear Future College Student,

I am assuming that as you read this letter, you are at a pinnacle stage in your life. You're getting ready to set off to college or venture off into the great unknown of "adulting." First off, I would like to say that taking the time to read these letters in the hopes of bettering yourself for the future is an absolutely incredible step for you to take. That being said, throughout our lives very few things will stay constant or consistent as we shift and transition through different phases— especially between the influential years from youth to adulthood.

But no matter the age, race, or gender, there are two constants that have been and always will be there:
God and money.

Looking at these two things, you may not see anything in common. You may even possibly perceive them as polar opposites. But that's actually a very common misconception. Before I go on, there are some of you who are probably thinking of the verse that says, "money is the root of all evil." It is one of the most quoted verses from the Bible, but one that many people get wrong. This verse is found in 1 Timothy 6:10, and it actually says: "For the love of money is a root of all kinds of evil. Some people, eager for money, have wandered from the faith and pierced themselves with many griefs."

Paul, one the most influential writers of the New Testament, didn't write about how people should be poor. He didn't say that if we DO have money, we're looked down upon for having it. No, he pointed out that if our love is for money and it distracts or takes us away from faith, that is where the true evil lies. You see, money and wealth are a blessing if used in the right ways. Our love and attention are to be solely focused on the One who is consistent to us—the one who gives us all that we have. And that is God. One way our love for the Lord can be shown is through our generosity toward those in need.

Generosity is the act of giving up one's own time or money to others around them. As a first-year college student, finances are one of the heaviest things to deal with as you're living life on your own. During the first half of the year when I was attending church on Sunday mornings, they would pass around buckets for the offering, and I would sit there thinking things like, "I have nothing to give here because I still need food for lunch," or "I need to pay for gas to get home." It was really just any excuse I could think of for not giving away my money. Now, don't get me wrong, I didn't have much to give, because I really was scraping the bottom of the barrel for the funds I did have. But the reality is, I wasn't being generous in any sense of the word. My mindset was to take what I could get and hold onto it for as long as possible. That's a very stingy and selfish mindset to have for a devoted follower of Christ (and not the best example of one, if you ask me).

As Christians, we are called to be generous and plentiful with what we have so that we may grow and gain from one another. I withheld what I had from the church and other people out of fear of not having enough money to do what I wanted to do. I was afraid of what I wouldn't have because of the money I would give away. What a lack of faith this is! How can we say that we believe in a God who fed the five thousand with a few loaves of bread and some fish, but remain *afraid that if we give a couple dollars to the church we won't be able to eat ourselves? Or maybe it's that we won't be able to go out to events or purchase the shoes we want because we had to give away some of our money. Hebrews 13:5 says, "Keep your lives free from the love of money and be content with what you have, because God has said, 'Never will I leave you; never will I forsake you.'"*

Do not think that because you are still in high school or because you live under your parents' roof that none of these verses apply to you. As far as I know, the Bible doesn't say anything about an age limit on living for God. Matthew 19:21 says,

"Jesus answered, 'If you want to be perfect, go, sell your possessions and give to the poor, and you will have treasure in heaven. Then come, follow me.'

Now, I may not be the greatest reader, but I don't see anywhere in that verse where it says you have to be an adult or on your own to be generous with the possessions you have been blessed with. Do not think that just because you are still under the authority of your parents or someone older than you that you can't start living the type of life you are called to live. Giving what we have and living with what we need is the most plentiful way to walk through life.

One last thought; just because your parents give to the church or give to people does not mean that you do! They are an example to follow and not a fast pass to get by when the offering comes around in service. You are your own person who lives by your own faith, and as such, you are called to make the decisions to better yourself for the future. This is not a guilt trip; it is simply a wakeup call—a friendly reminder that generosity in every sense of the word runs parallel to the love that we have for God.

Don't doubt what you can do with your generosity even at your age because God can use people of any age – at any time. The Bible has no age restriction on when we can start living like a Christian and neither should we.

Best wishes for your years to come.

You got this!

Cole Wheeler

If you won one million dollars today, what would you do with it?

I can't tell you the number of times I've been asked that question. Typically, I respond by saying something like, "I would buy a house for my parents." Then I start listing off all the places I would travel and all the nice things I would do for the people I love (including myself). But if you asked me the same question and replaced the million dollars with one hundred dollars, my response would be completely different. Isn't it funny how much easier it is to think about being generous when it seems like we have less to lose? But that's not how generosity works. You don't just become generous when you get rich. In fact, the more money you have, the easier it is to be selfish. Generosity is a muscle. It has to be developed, and you need to develop it for one simple reason: control.

Nothing has more potential to control you than money. That's why Paul said, "the love of money is a root of all kinds of evil." A desire, a need, or a love for money will only lead you to doing things to try and make more money. That's not to say you will rob a bank. You won't do that because it's illegal, and you won't get away with it, of course. You might however do something like rob a friend of an opportunity or compromise your standards to make more money.

Instead of letting money control you, you want to learn to control money. The easiest way to do this is to develop a habit now of giving it away. Thinking about this idea reminds me of Jesus' interaction with the rich young ruler.

As Jesus started on his way, a man ran up to him and fell on his knees before him. "Good teacher," he asked, "what must I do to inherit eternal life?"

"Why do you call me good?" Jesus answered. "No one is good—except God alone. You know the commandments: 'You shall not murder, you shall not commit adultery, you shall not steal, you shall not give false testimony, you shall not defraud, honor your father and mother.'"

"Teacher," he declared, "all these I have kept since I was a boy." Jesus looked at him and loved him. "One thing you lack," he said. "Go, sell everything you have and give to the poor, and you will have treasure in heaven. Then come, follow me."

At this the man's face fell. He went away sad, because he had great wealth.
- Mark 10:17-22 -

You see, the problem wasn't that the young ruler was rich. The problem was where he put his trust. Jesus wanted him to sell everything, to put his trust in Him and follow Him alone. But the ruler couldn't do that, because his trust was in his money. Wealth isn't the issue here; control is.

So, whether it's in giving to your local church or giving consistently to a non-profit you love, it's important to start stretching this generosity muscle now. And here's the kicker: It doesn't even matter how much you give. Start small. Give a little of what you have (and we all know you're about to not have a lot because… college). Give it to help the causes and the people around you. I promise you will never miss the money you give away to help others.

QUESTIONS

1. What churches or organizations could you start donating to?

_____

_____

_____

_____

_____

2. How much could you afford to give on a monthly basis?
    Be realistic here and remember, start small.

_____

_____

_____

_____

_____

3. How would giving help you take control of your money?

_____

_____

_____

_____

_____

ACTION STEP

Figure out how much you can afford to give on a monthly basis and set up an auto draft payment with one of the organizations you wrote down. (Hint: Auto draft is something you do from a bank account. Ask your mom, and she will help you!)

CHAPTER
EIGHT

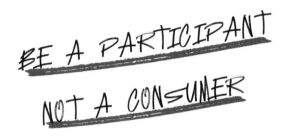

Q: Alright, I am picking up what you're putting down: pray and give. Is there anything else I can do to grow my faith in college?

A: Well, yes. And this one might be the most important of them all!

Dear Future College Student,

Your faith is going to change in college. The next four years of your life are pivotal for your spiritual walk with the Lord. That isn't to scare or pressure you to picture the perfect first year of college or make you believe that if it doesn't work out the way you hoped it would that then you're doomed. It's more to say that God is going to reveal more of Himself to you and teach you more about His heart and His people if you let Him in during that first year of college. You have the power to open a doorway for the Holy Spirit to come into your life like the wind. Whether that means finding a Christian community that encourages you, a club that glorifies your passions, or diving into a student ministry, do it with purpose.

Crazy enough, Jesus wanted us to be a part of His body. He wanted us to do life alongside other believers rather than on our own. To an extent, finding a home church in a new college town can be difficult. Sometimes you can fall in love instantly, while other times you don't find a fit right away. But, with patience and trust, you'll see that God really wants our faith to be about the final commission Jesus made: to make disciples by going into the world, spreading the Gospel, and being the hands and feet of God in your own community. What a blessing! Find something that you can participate in and saturate in it. You will be able to learn a lot of the characteristics of God through serving and loving His people.

Sometimes it's hard not to take up love from other people and decide to keep it to yourself. There are times when the easy way out may be to sit back and just take in what others (and God) are willing to give you. But you also have to get out there and give a little bit of yourself, too. Participate in the beauty that the Lord has planned for your life. Trust me, you don't want to miss it!

In all the billions of plans the Lord has perfectly crafted, the one He crafted for you is unique from the rest. It will be a testament to the faithfulness God has shown you and a testimony worth sharing. If you don't think that you have what it takes to lead others, serve well, and love uncontrollably, look back. Look at testimony after testimony of how God used your church and the people around you to lead you towards an abundant life. You never know when someone is looking for God to show up, and you could be the one to help Him do that for someone else. It could be through your service and love towards them that they begin to see God in a new way. Bring glory to the Lord and shout out His goodness! His sacrifice was too good to stay with us! Don't just consume but live it out and participate in the life Jesus died for us to have!

Sincerely,

Sam Short

In my first year of marriage, there is one thing I learned about myself: I am a consumer. In fact, I am a far better consumer than I am a participator. You know how I know this is true? Dinnertime. Any time my wife is cooking, I find myself in the kitchen standing over her shoulder and trying to pick at whatever she's making. When she's done, we sit at the table, and I devour the meal in about 7.9 seconds (give or take) before I go back in for another helping. Consuming is not a problem for me, clearly.

Participating is a completely different story. Again, the proof is right there at dinnertime. I have finished my meal by practically (okay, literally) licking my plate clean. I've eaten all the leftovers and am enjoying my state of fullness when my wife asks the question every husband hopes he never has to hear: "Babe, can you help me with the dishes?" Immediately, I start trying to think of ways to get out of helping her clean up the dishes that I have just attractively licked the crumbs from. As you can see in this case, when it comes to consuming, I am the first to enjoy. But when it comes time for participating, I am quick to find an excuse to do anything else. It is so much easier to receive what someone else is offering until they ask for your help, isn't it?

Consuming is easy. Participating requires work. Plot twist: Jesus did not call us to easy. He invited us to participate in His movement across the world. In fact, the last thing Jesus said to His followers when He was on Earth was a charge to participate in building the movement of Christianity. We know it now as the Great Commission:

*Then Jesus came to them and said, "All authority in heaven
and on earth has been given to me. Therefore go and make
disciples of all nations, baptizing them in the name of the
Father and of the Son and of the Holy Spirit, and teaching
them to obey everything I have commanded you. And surely I
am with you always, to the very end of the age."*
- Matthew 28:18-20 -

We have been called to participate in the sharing of the Gospel.
We've been called to be active parts of the body of Christ—His
church. Look at how Paul described the church:

*The body is a unit, though it is comprised of many parts.
And although its parts are many, they all form one body.
So it is with Christ. For in one Spirit we were all baptized
into one body, whether Jews or Greeks, slave or free,
and we were all given one Spirit to drink.*

*For the body does not consist of one part, but of many. If the
foot should say, "Because I am not a hand, I do not belong to
the body," that would not make it any less a part of the body.
And if the ear should say, "Because I am not an eye,
I do not belong to the body," that would not make it any
less a part of the body. If the whole body were an eye,
where would the sense of hearing be? If the whole body
were an ear, where would the sense of smell be?*

*But in fact, God has arranged the members of the body,
every one of them, according to His design.
If they were all one part, where would the body be?
As it is, there are many parts, but one body.*
- 1 Corinthians 12:12-20 BSB -

Paul said that we are all part of the body, and every part has something to offer to the whole. I don't know if you have ever thought about it that way or not, but you have something to offer that the church needs.

Of course, that doesn't make finding a church to attend easy. In fact, one of the most challenging decisions you will make in college is what church to attend. You will want to find a place you enjoy, a pastor who keeps your attention, and messages that challenge you. You want a church that can offer you everything you are looking for, and I get that. But the danger in that mentality is that it is consumer mentality.

I fear that when you go off to college and don't find a church that can offer you everything you are looking for, you may just decide it's easier to not attend one at all.

I want to challenge you to look at this differently. What if when you get to college, you look for the church you enjoy most and then ask how you can serve there? How can you participate in what God is doing in the local church?

I think if you start to participate in what the church is doing, you may end up finding a church you love because of how much you are a part of what's happening there. Instead of focusing solely on what you would be consuming from it, you're focusing on participating in what's happening in it. I really believe that if you are serving, you will find a great community and a home away from home in your new college town.

QUESTIONS

1. What are you looking for in a church home?

_____

_____

_____

_____

_____

2. Write down three churches to go visit in your college town.

_____

_____

_____

_____

_____

3. What is an area of the church you could serve in?

_____

_____

_____

_____

_____

ACTION STEP

Set dates to visit each of the churches you wrote down. Then, decide which one you want to get more involved in and find out more information about what it would look like to serve there. And I'm just sayin', I also hear church is a great place to meet your future spouse.

_____

_____

_____

_____

_____

_____

_____

CHAPTER
NINE

Q: This book seems to be a lot about adulting, but I don't even know what "adulting" is, really.

A: You're right. That's a weird word for a big idea. Let me try and help explain it.

Dear Future College Student,

I just want to start off by congratulating you on your accomplishment of (fingers crossed) finishing high school! This is one of the first real "growing up" moments in your life. I hope it feels amazing. I hope you can look back on your high school experience and be proud of the person you grew to be throughout your four years there. No matter if you've attended church since your freshman year or only went a few times, the lessons you've learned will last you a lifetime and continue to lay the foundation for your faith as you grow.

Whether you will be going off to college in the fall, joining the workforce, or taking off on a unique adventure, your life is about to change drastically. I don't want that to come across in a negative way, because it's not a negative thing at all. Leaving your comfort zone and getting a taste of what the real world is like is an incredible feeling. It's how most people find out what they want to do with their lives. Many of you will no longer live under your parents' roofs or follow the same schedules you had throughout high school. You will be thrown into a world of freedom, but with great amounts of freedom, comes an even greater amount of temptation. Although this can be intimidating, there is a truth here: The path your life takes is far more up to you than it is the world. Yes, there will be many things in your life beyond high school that try to pull you away from Jesus. But you need to know that you are more than capable of handling these distractions and using the struggles to fall deeper in love and trust for our Savior.

One of the absolute best things you can do as a young adult is stay involved in a church you love. It might not seem like it, but I assure you the adult service is your service. I imagine that most of you have attended an "adult" service at some point in your life. If you're anything like me, the messages may have flown right over your head sometimes, or they may have rung very true to your life at times. Whether you regularly attend adult services or have only been once or twice, I highly encourage you to attend them at a church you love, wherever you find yourself moving forward in life. Because attending these services forces you to grow. And, if you put in the just slightest amount of effort, you will grow exponentially. If you place yourself in these services, you are automatically surrounded by an older, wiser community that has been through exactly what you are going through in your life already—the wonderful things, the challenging things, the grown-up questions that don't necessarily line up with the faith you found in your high school service. All those questions will have the chance to be addressed either in the service or by the people you are surrounded by as you attend.

All in all, through my experiences moving away from my home, I have learned to allow myself to dive into what may seem intimidating for you right now as a soon-to-be graduate. Even though it may seem like a reach, you don't fit in, or the message seems too mature for you, keep investing and showing up in an adult service in college. There are few places that you can grow more than in the walls of a church you love. Find that, pray that the Lord leads you to a place you can belong, and become the adult Christ is calling you to be. The bigger the leap of faith, the more room God will have to work in your life. Invite Him in and watch how He provides for you. Go out into wherever you have been led and be a vessel for Christ. I promise, you are more than qualified.

Best regards,

Luke Wortman

If you've read through the last nine chapters, here is what you may have realized by now: You are already an adult. Ready or not, you're a grownup. You are months away from being out on your own. Months away from figuring out grocery shopping, bills, and scheduling one hundred percent on your own. And as you'll quickly realize, this newfound freedom is going to come with new responsibility. "Adulting" can be amazing, but it is also difficult, and if you are going to navigate all the decisions that come with this stage of your life, then you are going to need some guidance along the way.

Whether you think you're ready or not, it is time for you to hear from people who are talking about marriage even though you aren't married yet. You are going to need to hear from people who are talking about how to manage finances even though you won't have much money for the next four years. You are going to need to hear from people who are talking about adult issues. (You see where this is going.) My point is that the adult service is your service now, and the sooner you embrace that, the sooner you'll begin to learn from it.

The Bible never speaks to the transition from youth group to adult services, but it does talk about maturing in your faith. Look at what the writer of Hebrews said:

> *Anyone who lives on milk, being still an infant, is not acquainted with the teaching about righteousness. But solid food is for the mature, who by constant use have trained themselves to distinguish good from evil.*
> *- Hebrews 5:13-14 -*

The writer is basically saying this: There comes a point when we all must mature. We must go from milk to solid food. As you get older, the content you digest needs to get deeper; it needs to become more relevant to your stage of life. It should become harder for you to process as you get older.

How does that happen? Well, you transition. You start feeding yourself solid food. And while yes, that literally means a lot of *Ramen Noodles* and *Pop-Tarts*, spiritually it means more daily devotions through prayer, more going to church, more sitting under the teaching of people who are wiser and more experienced than you! I get it that it sounds boring! Trust me, I see students on their phones throughout my messages, too. Adult services may not seem applicable to you, but the good news is, this isn't trigonometry. What you'll hear in an adult service will at some point be useful, applicable, and actually even interesting to you. You just have to be willing to attend long enough for that to be the case.

If you've been waiting for someone to tell you, let it be me: This is the time to grow up! Start attending the adult service. If you can, go to both that and your local church youth group or college service. That way, you'll hear from someone speaking to where you are now and someone speaking to where you are going to be. When you get to college, find a campus ministry and if they don't have one, now you know that the adult service is your service.

You're a grownup; you have no excuses!

QUESTIONS

1. What makes you nervous about attending an adult service?

_____

_____

_____

_____

_____

2. What could you do to help make the content more applicable to you?

_____

_____

_____

_____

_____

3. Which churches have college ministries near your school that you could attend?

_____

_____

_____

_____

_____

ACTION STEP

Make a list of the dreams you have for your future (marriage, job, kids, etc.). Every time you go to an adult service, write down what you learned as it relates to those topics.

CHAPTER
TEN

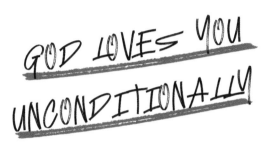

Q: Okay, this is a lot to take in. What if I screw this up?

A: I have one word for you: UNCONDITIONAL.

Dear Future College Student,

"Congrats, you made it! Get excited for the best four years of your life!"

I would imagine this is a phrase you've heard quite often during your current season. I hate to burst your bubble, but studies show that only 19 percent of incoming freshman actually finish school in four years. I'm not telling you that to discourage you; I'm telling you that because that would have been helpful for me to know going into college. Don't rush this next season of your life. Instead, enjoy every moment. Because whether it takes you four years or fourteen years, this season will serve as one of the most pivotal seasons in your entire life. You're going to have more fun than you can ever imagine, you're going to meet your lifelong friends, and you're going to begin to discover who you truly are.

But with that, I wish someone had told me how difficult my first year of college would be. I was so overwhelmed by how much "fun" everyone said I would have that I wasn't ready for the challenges that came with freshman year. But like anything in life, you have to take heart. Because in the end, it's both the good and bad moments that will make us truly appreciate the entire season.

Along the way, you're going to make mistakes. You wouldn't grow if you didn't. Don't be afraid of the mistakes you might make; be more afraid of not learning from them. In the end, that's what matters most.

If you're struggling with something, know that it's not who you are. It's just a part of you, something that can make you that much more relatable to someone who might be walking through a season very similar to yours one day. You don't have to have everything figured out or get all of your questions answered to rest in the promise that God loves you unconditionally. He has intentionally prepared the path before you.

It's easy to let mistakes define us and allow them to tell us who we are. Don't give them that much power. Luckily for us, our identity isn't found in the mistakes we make; our identity is found in the One who died on the cross for us.

Along your journey you are going to be tested, challenged, and questioned for everything you believe and every part of who you are. Don't be intimidated by their questions. Instead, allow people to be inspired by your response. Before I left for college, my mentor told me, "Don't get too comfortable with who you are right now, because in the next four years you're going to change more than you could ever believe."

If you're anything like me, I felt like I was on top of the world when I graduated high school. Nothing could compare or get better than life like it was right then... or so I thought. Fast-forward to now, three years into the four years he was referring to, and I have changed more than I could have ever imagined. Most people often associate change with something negative, but if there is anything I can encourage you with, it's to always look at change through the lens of positivity. In the next four years, you're going to change a lot, and that's what makes these years so special. You're going to discover new passions, *new dreams, and new experiences that will serve as the inspiration for who you aspire to become. You will experience seasons of hardship, celebration, confusion, and disappointment, but above all, seasons of gratitude as you reflect on where you've been and how far you've come.*

Always remember, when you're following God, you're exactly where you're supposed to be, doing exactly what you're supposed to be doing. Be proud of who you're becoming. People care more about the journey than the destination.

Excited for you,

Blake Eason

Unconditional is a hard word for us to understand because we live in such a conditional world.

So many of us only know conditional love. Conditional love says that if you behave the right way, then you'll be loved.

If you do what I want you to do, then I'll love you. If you buy me shoes, then I'll love you. (But really, if you buy me shoes I will love you. I wear a size 12.) But that kind of love—conditional love—is not a picture of God's love for us.

God's love for us is like the love of most parents to their children. But even that relationship can be hard to understand. Why? Because so many relationships between parents and children are tainted in our world today. With that, God's love for us can be really hard to understand. I will tell you that even I am personally still trying to understand this kind of love without condition. For me, this is hard to believe because of my dad. It wasn't until I was 26-years-old that I realized the real effect he had on me.

When you grow up either missing a parent or dealing with a parent who isn't quite ready to be one, it can really mess with your image of God. It makes it hard for you to understand that God really is always with you. It makes it hard for you to picture Him as a loving parent. It makes it hard to believe that He will love you no matter what.

That's been the story for me, and I know it probably has for many of you, too.

I need to be reminded of God's love for me often. I need to be told what it looks like. I bet you do as well. That is why I love the cross. The cross is our reminder that no matter how far we get, no matter how much we mess up, or no matter how many mistakes we make, we are never out of reach from God's love for us. Arguably, the most famous verse in the Bible puts it this way:

> *For God so loved the world that he gave his one and*
> *only Son, that whoever believes in him shall*
> *not perish but have eternal life.*
> *- John 3:16 -*

God loved, so God gave. He didn't give as a response to our good behavior. He didn't give because we earned it. No, God gave His Son in spite of our bad behavior. He gave us Jesus to demonstrate His love for us. So, what if you screw up? Just look back at the cross and let that serve as the reminder that you are and always will be unconditionally loved by your perfect Heavenly Father. Jesus is the picture of God's love for us, and it is His love that allows us to love God right back.

I guess this takes us back to the beginning where we started this whole thing. You see, your love for Jesus is a response to His love for you. As you pursue and run after Him, remember it is all because He first chose you.

QUESTIONS

1. What does unconditional love mean to you?

_____

_____

_____

_____

_____

2. Have you ever truly accepted the unconditional love of God?
    If not, what would that look like for you to do that now?

_____

_____

_____

_____

_____

3. How can you remind yourself that God loves you when you
    make a mistake?

_____

_____

_____

_____

_____

ACTION STEP

Take your answers from question three and create a plan to remind yourself of God's love for you.

_____

_____

_____

_____

_____

_____

_____

CHAPTER
ELEVEN

Q: Alright, I made it this far, and honestly, my senioritis is starting to kick back in. I don't think I've read this much since I checked Twitter this morning. Anything else you gotta say?

A: Before I leave you, let's just do a quick recap. And there is one more letter I want you to read.

So, there you have it: Ten things to know before you go. Ten things to help your faith grow. I hope that at the very least, these ten things have helped you reflect on all you've learned about yourself during high school and encouraged you in what God will continue doing through you as you move on to this next season.

I hope that the letters from real college students inspired you, eased your anxieties, and helped you realize that you don't have to go through this life alone.

Take a picture of this list and save it as the background on your phone for an easy reminder of the ten things to know before you go...

THINGS TO REMEMBER

1. Love Jesus more.
2. Do's over don'ts.
3. There's no such thing as a straight line.
4. Make new friends NOW.
5. Community doesn't happen by mistake.
6. Pray for strangers.
7. Generosity starts small.
8. Be a participant, not a consumer.
9. Adult service is MY service.
10. God loves ME unconditionally.

Will this make the next four years perfect? No, I can't promise that. But I do hope it will make them easier. I hope it will help you take some steps and make some decisions that will help your faith continue to grow in this next phase of your life.

I hope this will prepare you for reality, but also encourage you for the future. The next four years will be hard and incredible. They'll be challenging and unforgettable. God will teach you, mold you, walk with you, and grow you in ways you could never imagine. I can't wait to see how He uses you to change the world.

As promised, here is one last letter to read before you go.

Dear Future College Student,

You have no idea how much potential you have! I wish you could see it. I wish you could see how much you will change over the next four years. I wish you could see the influence you will have and the people you will impact. I wish you could see the plans God has for your future and the man or woman you are going to become.

But you can't see it. None of us can. We don't know what's ahead or what's to come, but there is something we can see: the past. I've heard it said not to look back, but to keep moving forward. I have to disagree with that.

I think there are moments in life where you have to stop and look back. This, right now, is one of those moments for you. Think about how far you've come. The fact that you have made it this far is a major accomplishment.

Think about high school for a minute. Think about the hours of studying you've done. The thousands of tests you've taken. The number of papers you "finessed" your way through. Think about your friends. The moments you've experienced. The fights that you've had. The friends you've gained and the ones you've lost. Think about your family. The things you've been through. The conversations that have been had. The sacrifices that have been made.

A lot has happened over the last four years, hasn't it? And look at you. You made it through. And you're still standing. God has used the last four years to shape you into the man or woman you are today. He has put people in your life that have helped guide you to this point. He has taken bad situations and used them for good (even if you can't fully see the result of that yet).

God has prepared a way for you and walked with you through every step of the journey. And if He's done that the last four years, why wouldn't He do it with you for the next four years and beyond?

Be assured of this, my friend: The journey ahead will not be walked alone. There may be moments you question that. There may be moments when you have doubts. There may be moments when you just want to quit. But know that even when you can't see it, God is there! He is fighting for you, cheering for you, and loving you every step of the way.

So, before you go, I just want you to know…

YOU ARE LOVED.
YOU ARE CHOSEN.
YOU ARE NOT ALONE.

Your friend,

Gerald Fadayomi

ACKNOWLEDGEMENTS

I have to start by thanking my incredible wife, Kiley Fadayomi. Thank you for reading the early drafts of the book, looking at what felt like 8000 different cover designs, but most of all thanks for being a constant encouragement and support to me.

To my family, Phil, Julie, Ryan, Drew and Caroline, thanks for being in my corner and having grace for me when I missed events and forgot things as I was finishing this book.

To my team at Browns Bridge InsideOut, thanks for being some of the best people I know. Thanks for believing in students and dedicating your life to help them grow in their relationship with Jesus. The concepts in this book come in large from watching the way you have invested in and mentored the students in our ministry.

To the students at Browns Bridge InsideOut, you are world changers! I can't wait to see how you will impact universities for the name of Jesus across the country.

To Reed Moore, Tim Benitez, Joseph Sojourner, Stuart Hall, and Grant Partrick, thanks for writing the video curriculum that makes this book more tangible for students.

To Nicole Bader Jones and Sarah Shelton, thanks for all the hours of editing you spent correcting my terrible grammar.

To Clay Scroggins, thanks for believing in me. You have shared knowledge and wisdom with me that you never had to. You are a leader worth following and I am grateful to know you and call you friend.

Finally, thanks to my little sister, Kelsey Davis, who is responsible for the look and feel of this project! You are a creative genius and I can't wait for our next project.

I am who I am today because of all of you. Thank you!